THE CHRISTIAN'S PRIMARY OBLIGATION

But seek ye first the kingdom of God and His righteousness.
MATTHEW VI. 33

Hugh Binning

Vintage Puritan Series
GLH Publishing
LOUISVILLE, KY

Sourced from *The Works of the Rev. Hugh Binning*.
Edited by M. Leishman. A. Fullarton and Co.: 1851.

ISBN:
Paperback 978-1-948648-47-9
Epub 978-1-948648-48-6

CONTENTS

Sermon I... 1

Sermon II. 15

Sermon III. 26

Sermon IV. 46

Sermon V.. 60

Sermon I.

"But seek ye first the kingdom of God and his righteousness," &c.
Matthew vi. 33.

This is a part of Christ's long sermon. He is dissuading his disciples and the people from carnal carefulness and worldly mindedness. The sermon holds out the Christian's diverse aspects towards spiritual and external things. What is the Christian's disposition in regard to the world, how should he look upon food, raiment, and all things necessary in this life? "Be careful for nothing." "Take no thought for your life, what ye shall eat, or drink," &c. "Seek them not as your chief good." But what is his disposition towards spiritual and eternal things, and how ought ye to look upon them? "Seek them, set your heart upon them, look upon them as your treasure, and where your treasure is, let your heart be there also." So then you see here two callings and employments of a man in the world,—two universal callings that comprehend all men, one natural to us, and unlawful, the other divine, and lawful, the one paganish, the other Christian. What is the employment of all men out of Christ? There are many different callings and employments among men. One spends his time and thoughts one way, and another another way, but all of them agree in one general, whatever they are: Their heart is here. The thoughts they have are bounded and circumscribed in this present world. They are careful for nothing else but what concerns their back and belly,[1] or their name and credit. Take the best of them, whose employment seems most abstracted from the common affairs and distractions among men, yet their affections run no higher than this present world. On the other hand, what should be the exercise and employment of a Christian? It is even this, whatever he be, or whatever his occupation be among men, he drives a higher trade with heaven, that should take him up. The world gets but his spare hours. He is upon a more noble and high project. He aspires after a kingdom. His heart is above where Christ is, and where his treasure is. And these things exhaust his affections and pains. Christ Jesus once takes the man's heart off these baser things, that are not worthy of an immortal spirit, let be[2] a spirit who is a partaker of a divine nature. But because the creature cannot be satisfied within itself, its happiness depends upon something without itself, (and this speaks out the vanity of the creature, and something of God, that is peculiar to him, to be self sufficient,) therefore Christ changes the object of the heart, and fixes the spirit upon a nobler and divine exercise. Since the spirit of a man cannot abide within doors without starving, it must run out upon something, therefore Jesus Christ hath described its bounds and way, its end and period. Before, a man sought many things, because not one was satisfying, that the want of one might be supplied by another; and therefore he was never near the borders of contentment and happiness, because still a

---

1 A proverbial expression signifying food and raiment. — Ed.

2 Much less. — Ed.

thousand things are wanting. But now, Christ puts the soul upon a satisfying and self sufficient object. And here the streams of affection may run in one current, and need not divide or go contrary ways.

First: We have here then the Christian's calling and employment in this world, opposed to the carefulness and worldly mindedness of the men of this world, "Seek ye the kingdom of God." *Secondly*: His encouragement and success in two things, one is expressed, the other implied. That which is expressed, is seeking the kingdom of God, of grace and glory. If ye seek this kingdom, all temporal things shall be laid to your hand, all these things that ye need "shall be added unto you." The other imported is, ye shall get the kingdom who seek it. For the words, "added unto you," suppose the first and principal intent to be gotten. Then the Christian's success and encouragement is this, ye shall have the thing ye seek and more also. It was said to Solomon, "Because thou hast sought wisdom, therefore thou shalt get all other things." Because, O Christian, thou sought the kingdom of God, and not this present world which Satan is prince of, therefore thou shalt get according to thy word, and thou shalt also get what thou asked not, 1 Kings iii. 11-13. He hath success in the main business, and there is a superplus besides, some accession to his portion, that comes of will, so to speak. The kingdom of God in the New Testament is sometimes restricted to the elect, the word of the gospel, and the administration of it, by the Spirit of grace in the hearts of his people. This is frequently called "the kingdom of heaven," and "of God," Matth. xiii. 33. Sometimes the kingdom of God is taken for the state of grace, a new principle of spiritual life, that grows up to the perfect day, and this kingdom is within us, Luke xvii. 21. It is taken also for heaven, the kingdom of glory, Luke xxii. 16. Both these must be sought after, (Luke xii. 31) and received, (Luke xviii. 17) and must suffer violence, Matth. xi. 12. The righteousness thereof may be taken for the righteousness of God by faith, Rom. x. 3, chap. iii. 21, 22, 2 Cor. v. 21, Rom. iv. 11, 13, Rom. ix. 30, chap. x. 6, Heb. xi. 7, Phil. iii. 9.

We would observe here: I. That the Christian's name and occupation is to be a wanter and a seeker. II. The great exercise and employment he should have in this world, that which should swallow up his affections, thoughts, and endeavours, should be the kingdom of God and his righteousness, which is clearly expressed in three things: 1. His first and chief care should be to be at peace with God, and to be adorned with Christ's righteousness; 2. To have the kingdom of God within him, a throne of judgment erected for Christ to rule the whole man, by his Spirit according to the word; 3. To be made an heir here, and a possessor hereafter, of the everlasting kingdom of glory; 4. No man can either be a subject of God's gracious kingdom here, or his glorious kingdom hereafter, without the imputed righteousness of the Son of God, and whoever seeks righteousness must also seek the kingdom of God. These are joined together, and there is a great opposition between seeking of the world, and seeking grace and glory. Whoever is careful in these things cannot be ent here. But rather seek the kingdom of God (Luke xii. 31) also implies, 5. That whatever a man be, or his profession be, except he seek this way of righteousness, and yield himself unto God's kingdom of grace, and unless Christ rule in him, he is but a pagan, or infidel Gentile, in God's account. We return to the first of these, namely:

1st. That the Christian is a seeker. This is the ordinary description of a child of God, Psal. xxiv. 6, Psal. xxvii. 8. Many, at this time, call themselves Seekers.[3] They profess they seek a true church, and seek ordinances purely dispensed, but find none. But the child of God, the good Christian that seeks according to Christ's appointment, seeks not these things as if they were not, but he seeks God in ordinances, he seeks Christ in the church, he seeks grace and glory, honour and immortality, and eternal life. He is in the church, he hath the ordinances rightly administered, yet he wants the most part, till he find Jesus Christ in all these. Many seek corn, wine, or any worldly good thing, saying, "Who will show us any good?" Fie upon such a lax and indifferent spirit, that hath no discretion or sense of things that are good, that sees not one thing needful, and no more good than is necessary. But the child of God is a seeker different from these also, he seeks the favour and countenance of God, Psal. iv. 6, 7. He seeks wisdom above all things, Prov. ii. 4. He seeks but one good thing, because there is but one good thing necessary. The seeking Christian is a wanter, one that hath nothing, and finds it so. He wants, and

---

[3] The sect of Seekers hold that there are not at this time, neither have been for many ages past any true ministers or ambassadors of Christ. (Gillespie's Miscellany Questions, p. 1. Edinburgh, 1649.) A few years before this, Laurence Clarkson, a *Seeker*, published a pamphlet entitled "The Pilgrimage of Saints." Edwards, in his Gangræna (Part I, p. 24, Part II, p. 6. London, 1646) refers to it for an account of the opinion of the Seekers. Clarkson declared that in these days there ought to be no churches built, no sacraments administered, that the saints as pilgrims, wander here as in a temple filled with smoke, not being able to find religion, and that, on this account, waiting for a church and for the coming of the Spirit as the apostles did, they ought to seek knowledge of any passenger, of any opinion or tenet whatsoever. — Ed.

knows he wants, else he would never seek. What wants he? Nay, rather ask, what hath he? It may soon be told what he hath, but it is hard to tell what he wants. Look what he hath, and ye find little or nothing, and therefore ye may conclude he wants all things. The text tells what he wants: (1) He wants righteousness; (2) He wants grace; (3) He wants glory, and hath no right to it. Men seek not what they carry from the womb. Therefore all men have come into the world with three great wants. (1.) Ye want righteousness. Ye cannot stand before God in the terms of strict justice. There is nothing ye have, or can do, but it is a menstruous cloth, Isa. lxiv. 6. All your religion and prayers will never commend you to God's holy justice. The scripture hath passed this sentence upon you all, "There is none righteous, no not one," Rom. iii. 10. The righteousness that the law of God requires is perfect, and complete, and exact. Either lay down the whole sum, or if it want a farthing it is no payment. Keep all the nine commands, but if ye break the tenth the nine will not suffice. Now all of you have sinned and corrupted your ways, and it is impossible to make up the want. As the redemption of the soul is precious and ceases for ever, so the broken and dyvour[4] man having become a bankrupt, shall never make up or pay his debt to all eternity. He hath once broken the command, and all your keeping afterwards will not stand for the obedience ye should always have given to it. Therefore sinners of the posterity of Adam, and wretched men by nature, see this great want and impossibility to recover it in yourselves. (2.) Ye likewise want all grace by nature. There is no

---

4 A name formerly given to bankrupts in Scotland.—See Act. James VI. par. 23, cap. 18.—Ed.

delusion more ordinary than this, that the world thinks grace is very common. But believe it, Sirs, that all men came from the womb without grace, get it as ye will. Look what the scripture speaks of the whole race of Adam, "There is no fear of God before their eyes," Rom. iii. 18. They are without Christ, without hope, and without God in the world, aliens from the covenants of promise, Eph. ii. 1-3, 12. Let grace be as common as can be, yet all of you once wanted it. Ye have it not by birth, nor by education, nor by baptism. Ye think perhaps a baptized soul cannot be graceless, but know it for a truth that ye have neither legal righteousness nor evangelical holiness. All of you have wofully fallen from righteousness, and therefore ye lie, with Adam's posterity, without hope in the world. Grace and truth must come from above by Jesus Christ; grace and glory are the gifts of God. (3.) The sinner also comes short of the glory of God, Rom. iii. 23. All sinners are born heirs of hell and wrath, without the hope of happiness. There is none born with a title to the kingdom of heaven, or any right to it. Man in his fall lost his right to eternal life and immortality, and hath purchased a doleful right to the Lord's wrath and to hell fire. Ye think it strange that any christened or baptized person should be damned, but the scripture knows no difference. "Neither circumcision nor uncircumcision availeth any thing, but a new creature, and faith which worketh by love." Neither to be a member of the visible church nor a pagan avails any thing, "for all have sinned and come short of the glory of God." Now what have ye since ye want righteousness? Ye want grace and ye want glory, and in the place of these ye have unrighteousness, all sin, all God's curses and wrath, and this makes up complete misery. In a word, ye want God and Christ, and this is all, and enough for all, Eph. ii. 12. Ye have, by nature, more sibness[5] with Satan, and nearer relation to him, than to God, and if ye want God, what can ye have beside? Your abundance is want. As all things are theirs who are Christ's, so nothing is theirs who are not God's. In short, there is not in all the creation such a miserable creature as man, whom God hath magnified and exalted above the angels, and the rest of the works of his hands. Now all men want these, but no man knows this but the Christian, whose eyes Christ hath opened, and to whom he hath given eye salve. Laodicea was blind and saw not, but she thought she was rich enough, when she had nothing, Rev. iii. 17, 18. The man, who will discourse well on all the miseries of this life, and human infirmities, may be ignorant of these things. There is no man but knows some want. But what is it he misses? Nothing but what concerns his present being and well being in this world, and so the world may supply it. But the Christian wants something this vain world will not make up. "Whom have I in heaven but thee? And there is none upon the earth I desire beside thee," says the soul that hath found God. And whom want I in heaven but thee? (Psal. lxxiii. 25, 26) says the soul that seeks God. He wants God's favour, and the light of his reconciled countenance, Psal. iv. 6. If ye ask him, what seek ye, what want ye in all the world? He answers, "And now. Lord, what wait I for?" My heart and "my hope is in thee," Psal. xxxix. 7. None needed ask at Mary, "Whom seekest thou?" Any body that knows her, knows her want. It is he, the Christ Jesus, and she thinks all the world should want him,

---

5 Kindred alliance.—Ed.

and seek him with her, and thinks no body should be ignorant of him; for she speaks to the gardener, as if there had been no other in the world, John xx. 15. But,

2dly. His wants put him to seeking, to diligence. He misses something, and O it is a great something, infinitely more than he is worth in the world! He wants being and well being. He thinks himself as good as lost, and he comes at length to some point of resolution, with the lepers of Samaria, (2 Kings vii. 3, 4.) "Why sit we here till we die? If we enter into the city there is famine, if we sit still we perish, if we go out we may find bread." And so the poor soul, with Mordecai and Esther, comes to this conclusion, "If I perish, I perish;" nothing but perishing as I am, I will go and seek salvation in Jesus Christ, and it may be I will find it. Who knows but he may turn again? Resolution is born a man at first a giant, it goes out to the utmost border of want the first day. Wanting makes desire, and desire, attended with some hope, makes up resolution and purpose, and when the soul is thus principled, then in the third room,[6] it comes forth to action. Desire and hope give legs to the soul for the journey, and now the wanting Christian ye shall find with his hand in every good turn, his feet in every ordinance. Ye shall find him praying, reading, and hearing. It is true, resolution is born a man, and practice is born but a child, and scarcely will come up in many years to the stature of resolution. Always[7] diligence and violence is the qualification of his practice, (Heb. xi. 6, Matth. xi. 12) and this is written upon his using of means,

---

6 Or, in the third place.—Ed.

7 Notwithstanding.—Ed.

"How love I the Lord! I am sick of love." The Christian's diligence in the use of means proclaims his earnest desire to obtain, whereas many a man's practice speaks but a coldrife and indifferent spirit. That is a neutral who cares not whether he obtain or miss. Some Christians have some missings of God, and spiritual things, but alas! their want, and sight of want, makes them twice miserable, because it puts not their hand to action. The slothful and sluggard's desire slays him, because his hands refuse to labour, Prov. xxi. 25. O! but he finds many difficulties in the way. Though he have half a wish, or a raw[8] desire after Christ, yet it never comes farther than a conditional wish. A beggar may wish to be a king. He comes to no purpose in it and therefore his way is called a hedge of thorns. Whereas a seeking Christian finds a plain path where he goes, Prov. xv. 19. The sluggard says, "There is a lion in the way, and a lion in the streets." He concludes upon the means and duties of religion before ever he try them, Prov. xxii. 13, Prov. xix. 24. How lazy is he! He will not bring his hand out of his bosom, when he hath put it in. Thus the lazy and secure Christian is a brother to a great waster, his desire consumes him. He hath no more religion than a spunk[9] of desire; and he sits down with this spark of his own kindling, and the life of religion thrives not upon his hand, Prov. xviii. 9, 12. His seeking must have violence with it, Matth. xi. 12. But we may also observe concerning the Christian, that he is,

3dly. Defined on this side of time as a seeker. In heaven he is an enjoyer, and he seeks no more;

---

8   A cold desire.—Ed.

9   That is a glimmering or slight degree of desire.—Ed.

for how can the ox low over his fodder? He sits down to eat the fruit and sweat of his labour, and well may he triumphantly say, as the ancient philosopher said, "I have found, I have found."[10] But here he is a seeker still. Whatever he miss, he is still a seeker, and whatever he find, he is yet a seeker. He is named not from his finding, but his seeking, not from his enjoyment or attainment, but from his endeavour and aim. Though he find righteousness in Jesus, and remission of sins, yet he is a seeker of grace; though he be justified, yet he seeks holiness. There are many who would seek no more of God than pardon of sin. Let him deliver them from hell, and they will trouble God with no more requests. Doth not some of your own consciences speak, that ye would seek no more from Christ than to be saved from an ill hour, and to be found in him; whereas Paul was not content with this, but made an holy gradation, as we read, Philip. iii. 8, &c. He desired to know the power of Christ's resurrection, and to be made conformable to him by any means; and now, when he is found in Christ, and justified, he counts not himself well, or perfect and complete, or to have attained that which he struggled earnestly for. Would not many be content with a Saviour, but they love not to hear of a

---

10 This was the exclamation of Archimedes the celebrated geometrician of Syracuse, (ευρηκα, ευρηκα), after discovering, when in the bath, a method of detecting the quantity of alloy, which a fraudulent artisan had mixed with the gold of Hiero's crown. (Plut. Mor. et Phil. Op. p. 1094.) An exclamation somewhat similar was uttered by Cicero, when, searching for the tomb of Archimedes in the neighbourhood of Syracuse he at length perceived it covered with thorns and brambles (Cic. Tusc. Quest lib. v. cap 23.) But if they had cause to be delighted, much more surely had Philip the apostle reason to be so when addressing Nathanael, he cried out in ecstasy—We have found him of whom Moses in the law and the prophets did write, Jesus of Nazareth, the son of Joseph! John i. 45.—Ed.

king to rule over them, nor of his laws to regulate their lives by? They love an imputed holiness, as well as righteousness. But the true seeker seeks grace within him. Though he be justified, or freed from guilt and condemnation, and have the righteousness of Christ to cover him, and though he should never come into condemnation for sin, yet he seeks the death and destruction of it in his soul, and the life of holiness implanted and perfected in his inward man. Though he is sure of heaven, yet he would have God's image upon his spirit, and whole man.

4thly. Whatever degree of grace he have or attain, yet he is still a wanter, and still a seeker. He counts not himself to have attained, or to be already perfect, but presses forward to gain the mark and prize of God's high calling, Phil. iii. 13, 14. He stands at no pitch, but forgets what is behind, and overlooks it, he thinks it not worthy to come in reckoning. There is still so much before his hand, that he apprehends it to be lost time to reckon what is passed. His aim is to perfect holiness in the fear of God. He endeavours to be holy as God is holy, who is the completest pattern of unspotted purity and uprightness, and to be holy in all manner of conversation. He goes from strength to strength, till he appear blameless before God; he seeks grace for grace, Psal. lxxxiv. 5-8. And truly the man who seeks the exact copy or pattern, Jesus Christ, who is gone before his people into heaven, and he who knows the spiritual command in all its dimensions, he will not say "I have found," but will still want more than he hath, and seek what he wants. There are some professors who have attained some pitch and degree, as it were, the first day, and never advance further. They have gotten a gift of prayer, some way of discharging duties, some degree in profession, and they want no more. Look on them some years after, and ye would say, they have sought no more. And truly he who seeks no more shall never be able to keep what he hath already, as a fire must soon die away if ye add not new fuel to it. Christians are not green in old age, because they have come to a pitch in their religion, and stand there. No, religion should not come to its stature hereaway.[11] This is but the time of its minority. Grace should be still on the growing hand. The grace of God is but a child here. Heaven and eternity make up the man. Glory is the man, who was once the child grace.

5thly. The good Christian is still a seeker till Christ be all in all, till he apprehend that for which he is apprehended. As long as he is in this world he is a seeker. Whereof, ye will say? Not only of more grace here, but of glory hereafter. Here he hath no continuing city, but he seeks one to come, Heb. xiii. 14. He is a pilgrim on earth, embracing the promises afar off, and seeking his country, even heaven itself, Heb. xi. 13, &c. All your present enjoyments in this world, your own houses and lands, would not make you think yourselves at home, if ye were Christians at the heart. Ye would miss consolation, ye would want happiness in the affluence of all created things. And therefore, Christians, do ye want nothing when all things go according to your mind? Is there no hole in your heart that a world cannot fill up? This is not well. Ye ought to seek a city, while ye are in your own country, and ye should never think yourselves at home till ye be in heaven. The Christian gets some taste of the fruits of the land, some clusters in the wilderness

---

11 In the present world. — Ed.

and house of his pilgrimage, and this makes him long to be there. This inflames the soul's desire, and turns it all in motion to seek that which was so sweet. If hope be so sweet, what shall the thing possessed be? If a grape brought a savour and taste so refreshful, what must the grapes plucked from the tree of life be, and the rivers of pleasures, which are at God's right hand, for evermore be? Sit not down then, Christians, upon your enjoyments, whether they be worldly or spiritual, but aspire to high things.

Sermon II.

"But seek ye first the kingdom of God," &c.
Matthew vi. 33.

II. The Christian's chief employment should be to seek the kingdom of God, and the righteousness thereof. "Seek first," &c. Upon this he should first and chiefly spend his thoughts, and affections, and pains. We comprehend it in three things. *First*, He should seek to be clothed upon with Christ's righteousness, and this ought to take up all his spirit. This is the first care and the chief concern. Did not this righteousness weigh much with Paul, when he counted all things but loss and dung, that he might be found in Christ, not having his own righteousness, but the righteousness which is by faith in Jesus Christ? Phil. iii. 8, 9. Now this righteousness is of more concernment than all the world beside. For it is God's righteousness, (Rom. x. 3, 4; 2 Cor. v. 21.) and this holds out a threefold excellence in it. (1.) It is God's righteousness, because he alone devised it, and found it out. All the world could not have imagined a way possible to save lost mankind, or ever one sinner of that wretched number. Satisfaction to justice was needful, and there was none righteous among Adam's posterity. But here God himself in his everlasting counsel hath found it out, and all hath flowed from his love. The mission of Jesus Christ to be the propitiation for our sins, comes from this blessed fountain, 1 John iv. 9, 10; Rom. iii. 24, 25. God hath been framing this righteousness from all eternity, and even this world seems to be made for this end. All God's dispensation with Adam, his making a covenant of works with him, his mutability and liableness to fall, and so governing all things in his holy providence that he should fall from his own righteousness, and involve all his posterity in the same condemnation with himself,—all this seems to be in respect of God's intention and purpose, even ordained for this end, that the righteousness of Jesus Christ might be commended to you, far more than all the dispensation of the law upon Sinai, more than the curse and the command, the thunder and the lightning. The very condemnation of the scripture was all in God's own mind and revealed will also, as the means appointed to lead sinners to this righteousness, Rom. x. 4. Therefore, how precious should that be to us, that God keeps and preserves the world for?

(2.) By this righteousness alone, we can stand before God, and therefore it is termed God's righteousness; and is not this enough to make it lovely in the eyes of all men? This is the righteousness without the law, though it was witnessed both by the law and the prophets. This is the only righteousness that justifies, when all men are found guilty before God, Rom. iii. 19, &c. Now, what is it in this world can profit you, if ye want this? Condescend[12] upon all your pleasures and heart-wishes, let you have them all, and now, poor soul, pray what hast thou? Though thou hast gained the world, thou losest thy soul, that thou should use the world with? Let you then get what you so eagerly pursue in the world, what will ye do when

---

12 Specify or enumerate.—Ed

your soul is required by the hand of justice? "Then whose shall these things be?" Luke xii. 20, 21. By all these things, a man neither knows love nor hatred, as Solomon speaks of external enjoyments, Eccles. ix. 1. But hear the way, O men! how ye may stand before God; here it is only. Will it profit you to enjoy the world, and bless God? And when all these things leave you, and ye leave them, what will ye do,—for riches will not go to the grave with you? All that is here cannot help you in that day, when ye must stand before the Judge of all flesh. If a man be not found in Christ he is gone, and if he be found in him, then the destroying angel passes by, death hath a commission to do him good, God is become his friend in Jesus. If ye could walk never so blamelessly in this world, all this will not come as righteousness in God's sight, nor stand before him. It is only the righteousness of Christ that can be a covering to sinners. But,

(3.) This is God's righteousness, because it is the righteousness of Christ who is truly God, and so it is divine. This is the most excellent piece in all the creation, that comes from Jesus Christ, his life, death, and resurrection. And let all men's inherent holiness blush here and be ashamed. Let all your prayers, good wishes, your religious obedience be ashamed, let them vanish as the stars before the sun. The righteousness of Christ is the bright sun that makes all the dim sparkles of nature, civil honesty, and even religious education, disappear. Let even angels blush before him, for they are not clean in his sight, but may be charged with folly. Innocent Adam was also a glorious creature, but the second Adam, the life-giving Spirit and the Lord from heaven, hath an infinitely transcendent and supereminent excellency and prerogative beyond him, and all the creation of God. Look then upon this Jesus how he is described, as the "brightness of the Father's glory and the express image of his person," (Heb. i. 1-3; Col. i. 15, &c.) and wonder that such a glorious one should become our righteousness, that he should take our sins upon him, (2 Cor. v. 21; 1 Pet. ii. 24) and make over his righteousness to us. This is the righteousness of the saints in heaven, Rev. xix. 8. This is the glory of the spirits of just men made perfect. Think ye, my friends, that the glorious saints shall wear their own holiness upon their outside in heaven? No, no, the righteousness of Christ shall cover them, and that shall be the upper-garment that all the host of heaven must glory in. Now this is the thing that the child newborn, if he had the use of reason, should first cry for, before he ever get the breast, to be reconciled to God in Christ. Would ye then spend your time and thoughts upon other things, if ye knew what need ye have of his righteousness, and how suitable it were to your need? Should not the beggar seek food and clothing? Should not the sick man seek health, and the poor man riches? Here they are all in Christ's righteousness. Ye are under the curse of God. This righteousness redeems from the curse. Ye are sinners, and none of you righteous, no not one. But Christ was made sin for us, that we might be made the righteousness of God in him. O sinners, wonder at the change! Hath Christ taken on your sins, that his righteousness might become yours, and will ye not do so much as seek it? But many a man beguiles his own soul, and thinks he seeks this righteousness in the gospel. Therefore ye would know what it is to seek his righteousness. If ye seek it, ye want your own righteousness. And who of you have come this length, to judge yourselves that ye be not judged? It is a great difficulty to convince the multitude of sin. That general notion, that we are all sinners, is but the delusion that many souls perish in. Never any will deny themselves to seek another righteousness, till they be beaten and driven out of their own. There is need of submission to take and receive this righteousness, let be to seek it, And now tell me, can ye say that ye have seen all in yourselves as dung and dross, that ye count all things but loss for the excellency of the knowledge of Christ Jesus, (Phil. iii. 8, 9.) that ye have seen all your own privileges and duties loss, and are ye even sensible that prayer will no more help you than the cutting off a dog's neck? Ye that lay so much weight upon your being baptized, and upon outward privileges, are ye void of righteousness? No, ye seek to establish your own, and do not submit to the righteousness of God. In a word, all who are ignorant of this righteousness of God in Christ, ye all seek to establish your own. There needs more. But not one of twenty of you can tell what this is, it is a mystery. Ask at any of you, how ye shall be saved, ye will say, by prayer to God, and the mercy of God. Ye cannot tell the necessity of Christ's coming into the world.

Secondly, Ye must see an impossibility to attain a righteousness, or to stand before God another way. When ye miss this righteousness and are convinced of sin, it is not the running to prayer will help or mend it. When ye see the broken covenant, ye fall upon doing something, to mend your faults, with some good turns, and some will make a few good works answer all the challenges of sin. Alas! this is a seeking of your own righteousness. Many a poor broken man seeks to make up his fortune. Poor wretched sinners are building up the breach of the old covenant, putting up props under an old ruinous house, seeking to establish it, and rear it up again. But ye will never seek Christ till ye cannot do better, till ye be desperate of helping yourselves without him. Now I appeal to your consciences. Who among you was ever serious in this matter, to examine your own condition, whether you were enemies or friends? Ye took it for granted all your days. But never a man will betake himself to an imputed righteousness, but only he that flies, taking with[13] his enmity, and is pursued by the avenger of blood, and flies in to this righteousness as a city of refuge.

Thirdly, Ye must seek this righteousness, and what is it to seek it? It is even to take it and to receive it. It is brought to your door. It is offered. And the convinced sinner hath no more to do but hearken, and this righteousness is brought near unto him. Prayer to God, and much dealing with him, is one of the ways of obtaining this righteousness. But coming to Jesus Christ is the comprehensive short gate,[14] and therefore it is called "the righteousness of faith," and "the righteousness of God by faith." Now shall ye be called seekers of Christ's righteousness, who will not receive it when it is offered? Ye who have so many objections and scruples against the gospel and the application of it, ye in so far are not seekers, but refusers of the gospel, and disobedient. Christ's righteousness should meet with a seeker not a disputer. Any thing God allows you to seek, certainly he allows you to take and receive it, when it is brought unto you. And

---

13 Acknowledging.—Ed.

14 Path or way.—Ed.

therefore, whoever have need of Jesus Christ, not only refuse him not, but stay not till they find him come to them. This is a noble resolution, I will give myself no rest till I be at a point in this. Seek him as a hid treasure, as that which your happiness depends upon.

(1) The kingdom of grace is worthy of all your affections and pains. That despised thing in the world called grace is the rarest piece of the creation, and if we could look on it aright, we would seek grace, and follow after it. Grace extracts a man out of the multitude of men that are all of one mass. Grace separates him from the rest of the world, and to this purpose are these usual phrases in scripture, "Such were some of you," "Once ye were darkness, but now are ye light in the Lord," "Among whom ye had your conversation in times past, fulfilling the desires of the flesh." All men are alike by nature and birth, there is no difference. Grace brought to light by the gospel makes the difference, and separates the few chosen vessels of glory and mercy from the world, and now "they are not of the world, as I am not of the world." All the rest of men's aims and endeavours cannot do this. Learning makes not a man a Christian. Honour makes not a man differ from a Gentile or Pagan. Riches make you no better than infidels. Speak of what ye will, you shall never draw a man entirely out of the cursed race of Adam, never distinguish him from Gentiles before God, till the Spirit of regeneration blow where he listeth. And this is grace's prerogative, beyond all other things. All other excellent gifts, even the gift of preaching, praying, all these are common, so to speak, and in a manner befall to all alike. Your external calling is but common, but he gives grace to all his chosen

ones. But (2) grace puts a man in a new kingdom. It draws a man out of Satan's kingdom, and makes him a king, who before was a subject. The man was led captive by sin and Satan at their pleasure. He served his own corrupt lusts and the prince of this world. Sin reigneth in his mortal body, whatever his passion and corruption did put him to, he could have no bridle, but as a horse went on to the battle. And ye may see daily that there is scarce one of an hundred that is master of himself. He is a servant of sin, but grace makes him a priest and a king, Rev. i. 6, chap. v. 8, 10. He can now command himself. Sin reigned before unto death, but now grace reigns through righteousness unto eternal life, Rom. v. 20, 21. And O! but this victory over a man's self is more than a man's conquering a strong city. This victory is more than all the triumphs and trophies of the world's conquerors. For they could not conquer themselves, the little world, but were slaves to their own lusts. Some men talk of great spirits that can bear no injury. Nay, but such a spirit is the basest spirit. The noble spirit is that spirit which can despise these things, and be above them. Grace puts men upon a throne of eminence above the world. The Spirit of God makes a man of a noble spirit. (3) Grace translates a man from Satan's kingdom to God, and makes him a subject, a free born subject, of God or Christ's kingdom, and therefore Christ is the "King of saints," Rev. xv. 3. Our Lord and Saviour hath an "everlasting kingdom," 2 Pet. i. 11. We were subjects of the powers of darkness, but grace makes the translation into the kingdom of God's own dear Son, Col. i. 13. Now what an unspeakable privilege is this, to be one of Christ's subjects, who is our dear Saviour and King! Surely we must all be great courtiers. David, the great king of Israel, had this for his chief dignity, his style of honour, "the servant of the Lord," as kings use to write down themselves; and this was his title, "servant of God." Paul gloried much in this, "Paul, an apostle and servant of Jesus Christ." And surely all the families of heaven and earth may think it their highest honour to get liberty to bow their knees to Jesus, the "King of kings, and Lord of lords," the first-born of God's creation. The converted man is turned from the power of Satan to God. Mark but the emphasis of these two terms. Mark the whence or from, — that it is from Satan, the great destroyer of mankind, the first transgressor and deceiver. And how great is his power, tyranny, and dominion! He had us all in chains reserved for the day of judgment. But to what a happy change grace turns us, *from* him! But the term *to*, which is more admirable, it is to God, to Christ, to true religion, to God himself most High. And O! but this must be a more wonderful and excellent change than our conversion from darkness to light, from hell to heaven. These are but shadows of this glorious conversion. (4) Grace makes a man likewise a "partaker of the divine nature," 2 Pet. i. 4. This is the image and glory of God. This is the imitation and resemblance of God's spotless holiness and purity, "Be ye holy, as I am holy," 1 Pet. i. 15, 16. Every creature hath some dark characters of God. Some things speak his power, some things his wisdom, but this he hath called his own image. And so the Christian is more like unto God than all the world beside. This is the magnifying of a man, and making him but "a little lower than the angels," Psal. viii. 3, 4. Therefore God loves grace better than all the creation. Holiness is a great beauty, and God requires to be worshipped in the beauties of it. Albeit grace be often clouded with infirmities, and sometimes is reckoned despicable, because of the vessel it is in, yet it is precious as the finest gold, and more precious than any rubies. It is like gold in ashes, not the less excellent in itself, though it appear not so. But sin is the devil's image and likeness, and therefore Satan is called the father of sinners. "Ye are of your father the devil, and the lusts of your father ye will do." O but sin hath an ugly shape! It is the only spot in the face of the creation which God's soul abhors. For he loves righteousness, and hates iniquity, Psal. xlv. 6, 7. But there is one thing more, (5) that may commend grace to all your hearts. Grace is the way to glory. It gives title and right to, or at least declares it. It is inseparably joined with it. Grace is glory in the bud, and glory is the flower of grace, grace is young glory, and glory is old grace. Without holiness it is impossible to see God's face in peace. No man can come unto heaven without grace. Glorification is the first link of the chain, Rom. viii. 30. But sanctification must intervene first. No unclean thing can enter into heaven, but he that gives grace, gives glory, Psal. lxxxiv. 11. Heaven cannot receive many of you, because ye have not holiness. But it may commend holiness unto you, that it ministers an abundant entrance "into the everlasting kingdom of our Lord and Saviour Jesus Christ." As much as eternity is beyond the poor span of your time, so much is grace and holiness, whereon depends your everlasting condition, preferable to all things of this present vain world. O! but the children of men have many vain pursuits of the creature, that when it is had is nothing and vanity. Ye labour to secure an inch of your being, and to have contentment here in this half day, and never look beyond it to many millions of ages, when ye are to continue. Your honour, your pleasure, your gain, your credit, many such things like these can have no influence on the next world. These cannot go through death with you. Only grace and holiness, begun here, are consummated in glory, and make the poor man, that was miserable for a moment, eternally happy.

Sermon III.

*"But seek ye first the kingdom of God, and his
righteousness, and all these things shall be
added unto you."*
Matthew vi. 33.

The perfection even of the most upright creature, speaks always some imperfection in comparison of God, who is most perfect. The heavens, the sun and moon, in respect of lower things here, how glorious do they appear, and without spot! But behold, they are not clean in God's sight! How far are the angels above us who dwell in clay! They appear to be a pure mass of light and holiness, yet even these glorious beings cannot behold this light without covering their faces. These God may charge with folly. "God is light," saith the apostle, 1 John i. 5. This is his peculiar glory, for "in him there is no darkness at all." Is there any thing more excellent and divine than to seek God, and find him, and enjoy him? Yet even that holds forth the emptiness of the creature in its own bosom, that cannot be satiated within, but must come forth to seek happiness. Nay, even the greatest perfection of the creature speaks out the creature's own self indigence most, because its happiness is the removal from itself unto another, even unto God the fountain of life.

Now the enjoyment of this "kingdom of God" mentioned in the text, holds forth man's own insufficiency for well being within himself. But seeking this kingdom declares a double want, a want of it altogether. Not only hath he it not in himself, but not at all, and so must go out and seek it. God is blessed in himself, and self sufficient, and all sufficient to others. Without is nothing but what has flowed from his inexhausted fulness within, so that, though he should stop the conduit, by withdrawing his influence, and make all the creatures to vanish as a brook, or a shadow, he should be equally in himself blessed. "Darkness and light are both alike to thee," says David in another sense, Psal. cxxxix. 11, 12. And indeed they are all one in this sense, that he is no more perfected and bettered, when all the innumerable company of angels, and the spirits of just men made perfect, follow him with an eternal song, nor[15] before the mountains and hills were, when nothing was brought forth. Many thousand more worlds would add nothing to him, nor diminish anything from him. It is not so with man, he is bounded and limited, he cannot have well being in his own breast. He was indeed created with it in the enjoyment of God, which was his happiness, so that he had it not to seek, but to keep, he had it not to follow after, but to hold it still fast. But now, alas! he hath lost that, and become miserable. Once all Adam's posterity were void of happiness. By catching at a present shadow of pleasure, and satisfaction to his senses, he lost this excellent substance of blessedness in communion with God. Now, how shall this be recovered again? How shall this pearl of great price be found?

Certainly we must agree upon two principles, and according to them walk, ere we come within reach of this. It is a great question that is of more

---

15 Than.—Ed.

moment than all the debates among men,—how shall man's ruin be made up, and the treasure be found? If ye think it concerns you, I pray you hearken to this, and condescend[16] upon these two grounds, that the question may be right stated. One is, we have all lost happiness, fallen from the top of our excellency into the lowest dungeon of misery. We are cast down from heaven to hell. There needs not much to persuade you of the truth of this in general. But alas! who ponders it in their hearts? And until ye think more seriously upon it, ye will never be serious in the search for reparation of it. All of you by your daily experience find that ye are miserable creatures. Ye have no satisfaction nor contentment. Ye are compassed about with many infirmities and griefs. But this is but an appendix of your misery. All the calamities of this life are but a consequent, a little stream of that boundless ocean of misery that is yet insensible to you. Therefore enter into your own hearts, and consider what Adam once was, and what ye now are, nay, what ye will all quickly be, if God prevent it not. We are born heirs of wrath and hell. It is not only the infinite loss of that blessed sight of his face for evermore, which an eternal enjoyment of creature pleasures could not compensate the want of, one hour; but it is the kingdom of darkness, and the devil that we are all born to inherit. Let this then once take root in your heart, that ye are in extreme misery, and that a remedy must be provided, else ye must perish. Now when this principle is established, ye must agree upon this also. "But out of myself I must go. Blessedness I must have. It is not in me. While I look in, there is nothing but all kind of emptiness, and, which is

---

16 Fix upon.—Ed.

worse, all kind of misery. Not only the common lot of creatures (that none is sufficient to its own well being) is incident to me, but I have lost that being which I had in another, which was my well being, and do now possess, or shall shortly possess, all misery." Now, are ye settled upon these two? I am not happy, I must go out of myself to find it. It is not in me, in my flesh dwells no good thing, in my spirit and flesh both, is nothing good. Ask then this great question, Whither shall I go? What shall I do to find it? All men know they must seek it. But Christ tells where they shall seek it, and whither they shall go. The word of the gospel is for this very purpose to answer this question. If we were sensible that we had lost happiness, certainly we would be earnest in this question, where shall it be recovered? What shall I seek after? And no answer would satisfy but the gospel itself, that directs unto the very fountain of life, and holds "forth the kingdom of God" as the true happiness of men to be sought. "Seek ye first," says Christ, "the kingdom of God," and the righteousness thereof. Here only is a solid answer. Seek me, for I am eternal life, I am the life and the light of men. Oh! that your souls answered, with David, "Thy face, Lord, I will seek." Peter had sought and found, and thought himself well, so that he answers Christ with great vehemency, when he said unto his disciples, "Will ye also leave me?" Peter saith, Leave thee, Lord, "to whom should we go but unto thee, for thou hast the words of eternal life? And we believe and are sure, that thou art the Christ, the Son of the living God," John vi. 66, &c. It were all the absurdity in the world to leave thee, or to go to any other thing for life itself. Shall not death be found, if I leave life? It were madness not to seek thee, but what shall it be called to leave thee, when I have found and tasted thee to be so good? Every man misses happiness and justification within himself, and so is upon the search after it. But is it not strange, that all the experiences of nations and generations conjoined in one, cannot hold forth even a probable way of attaining it? Gather them all in one, the sum and result is, "We have heard the fame thereof with our ears," but "it is hid from the eyes of all living," as we read more fully, and should apply, what Job said of wisdom, to the true happiness of man, Job xxviii. 12, to the end of that chapter. Certainly there is some fundamental and common mistake among men. They know not what was once man's happiness, and so it is impossible they can seek the right remedy. Look upon us all, what do we seek after? It is some present thing, some bodily and temporal thing, that men apprehend their happiness lies in, and so whether they attain it or not, or being attained, it doth not answer our expectation, and thus still are we disappointed, and our base scent becomes a vain pursuit, whether we overtake it or not. Every man proposes this within himself as the principle of his life and conversation, what shall I seek after? What shall I spend most of my time and affections upon, to drive at? And alas! all men, save those whose eyes the Spirit openeth, err in the very foundation. One man propones honour to himself, another pleasure, and a third riches, and the most part seek all of them, some accommodation and satisfaction in a present world. And almost every man conceives he would be blessed, if he had that which he wants, and sees another have.

Now while men's designs are thus established, all must be wrong. The ship is gone forth, but it will never land on the coast of happiness. And thus we see men seek many things. They are divided among many thoughts and cares, because no one thing is found that can satisfy, and so we have put ourselves upon an endless journey to go through all the creatures. Neither one nor all together have what we want, and neither one nor all can be had or possessed with assurance, though we had it. But the gospel comes to lay a right foundation, and frame a right principle within us. "Seek ye first the kingdom of God." Here is the principal design that should be driven at and if men would make it, and follow it, O how should they be satisfied with the fulness of that kingdom, the vast dimensions of it, the incorruptibleness of it!

Now there is one of two you must fall upon, either many things, or one thing. All that a man can seek after is here ranked. On the one side is many things, "all these things," that is, food, raiment, honour, pleasure, and such like, that concern the body, or men's condition here in this world, and these things a man hath need of, verses 31 and 32, "Therefore take no thought, saying, What shall we eat? or, what shall we drink? or, wherewithal shall we be clothed? (for after all these things do the Gentiles seek) for your heavenly Father knoweth that ye have need of these things." Nay, there is but one thing that is set up against all these many things, namely, "the kingdom of God and his righteousness." Now without all controversy the more unity be, there will be the more satisfaction. If all other things be equal, it is a kind of torment to have so many doors to go to for help. If a man could have all in one, he would think many things a great vexation and burden. If any one thing had in it as much as to answer all our necessities, that one thing would be of great price, beyond many things, having but so much virtue among them all. I shall suppose then, that there were real satisfaction and happiness to be found in the affluence and conjunction of all created things here, that there was some creature that could answer every necessity of men, yet, I say, would ye not exchange all that variety and multitude, if ye could find one thing that did all that to the full, that so many did but no more? Then certainly ye would choose a variety in one thing beyond the scattered satisfaction in many things. But when it is not to be found in all these things, and though it were, yet all these are not consistent together, then of necessity we must make another search. I say then, in the name of Jesus Christ, that if ye seek satisfaction in this present world, ye shall be disappointed. Ye may be all your days sowing and ploughing, but ye shall not see the harvest. Ye shall never reap the fruit of your labour, but in the end of your days shall be fools, and see yourselves to have been so, when ye thought yourselves wise. I shall also suppose that ye have attained what ye have with so much vexation toiled for, that ye had your barns and coffers full, that all the varieties of human delights were still attending you, that ye were set upon a throne of eminency above others, and in a word, that ye had all that your soul desired, so that no room was left empty for more desire, and no more grief entered into your hearts. Are ye blessed for all that? No certainly, if ye do but consider that with all ye may lose your own souls, and that quickly, and that your spirits must remove out of that palace of pleasure and delight into eternal torment, and then count, are ye blessed or not? What gained ye? It is madness to reckon upon this life, it is so inconsiderable when compared with eternity. A kingdom, what is it, when a man shall be deprived for evermore of the kingdom of God, and inhabit the kingdom of darkness under the king of terrors? Do ye think a stageplayer a happy man that for an hour hath so much mirth and attendance, and for all his lifetime is kept in prison without the least drop of these comforts? Will not such a man's momentary satisfaction make hell more unsatisfying, and add grounds of bitterness to his cup? For it is misery to have been happy.

Nay, but this is a fancied supposal. All this, how small soever it be, was never, and never shall be, within the reach of any living. Ye may reckon beforehand, and lay down two things as demonstrated by scripture and all men's experience. One is,—all is vanity and vexation of spirit under the sun. All that ye can attain by your endeavours for an age, and by sweating and toiling, will not give you one hour's satisfaction, without some want, some vexation, either in wanting or possessing. Nay, though you had all, it could not give you satisfaction. The soul could not feed upon these things. They would be like silver and gold, which could not save a starving man, or nourish him as meat and drink doth. A man cannot be happy in a marble palace, for the soul is created with an infinite capacity to receive God, and all the world will not fill his room. Another is,—that it is impossible for you to attain all these things. One thing is inconsistent with another, and your necessity requires both. Now then, how shall ye be satisfied when they cannot meet? I think, then, the spirits of the most part of us do not rise very high to seek great things in this world, we are in such a lot among men. I mean that we have not great expectation of wealth, pleasures, honours, or such like. Oh then so much the more take heed to this, and see what ye resolve to seek after! Ye do not expect much satisfaction here. Then I pray you hearken to this one thing, seek the kingdom of God.

This kingdom of heaven and righteousness are equivalent unto, nay they exceedingly surpass, all the scattered perfections and goodness among these many things, or all things that God hath promised to add to them in the text. Why should I say equivalent? Alas, there is no comparison. "For I reckon (says Paul, Rom. viii. 18, 19) that the sufferings of this present time are not worthy to be compared with the glory that shall be revealed in us. For the earnest expectation of the creature waiteth for the manifestation of the sons of God." What this kingdom is in itself, is beyond our conception, but all these things which God will add thereunto, are to be considered only as an appendix to it. Is not heaven an excellent kingdom? All that ye are now toiling about, and taking thought for, these, "all these things" (as a consequent to itself), food and raiment, and such like, "shall be given you" as your heavenly Father judges fit. "For godliness (says the apostle, 1 Tim. iv. 8), is profitable unto all things having the promise of this life," as well as of "the life to come." I think then, if all men would but rationally examine this business, they would be forced to cry out against the folly and madness of too many men, who have their portion only in this life, Psal. xvii. 14. What is it ye seek? Ye flee from godliness as your great enemy. Ye think religion an adversary to this life, and the pleasures of it. Nay, but it is a huge mistake, for it hath the promise of this life, and that which is to come. Ye cannot abide to have Christ's kingdom within you. Ye will not have him to rule over you. Ye will not renounce self, and your own righteousness. But consider, O men, that here is that which ye should seek after. Here is wealth, and honour, and long life, and pleasures at God's right hand for evermore. Ye seek many things first, and ye will not seek this one thing needful, Luke x. 41, 42. But here is the way to get what ye seek more certainly and solidly, "Seek first the kingdom of God and his righteousness," and all these other things will come of will. Ye need not seek them, for your heavenly Father knows best what ye need. Behold what a satisfying portion this kingdom is. When the pitch and height of men's attainments in this world is but a consectary, an appendicle of it, what must this kingdom be in itself, when all these things follow as attendants? Here then is one thing, worth all, and more than all, even Jesus Christ, who is all in all, Col. iii. 10, 11. Ye speak of many kingdoms, nay, but here is one kingdom, the kingdom of grace and glory, that hath in it eminently all that is scattered among all things. It unites us to Jesus Christ, "in whom all the fulness of the Godhead dwells, and ye are complete in him, who is the head of all principality and power," Col. ii. 9, 10. In his house is fatness, and ye shall be satisfied with this, and drink of these rivers of everlasting pleasures that are at his right hand, Psal. xxxvi. 8, 9, xvi. 11. When the pious Psalmist was over-charged with the very forethought and apprehension of this, he says, "How excellent is thy loving kindness, O God! therefore the children of men put their trust under the shadow of thy wings," Psal. xxxvi. 7. "O how great is thy goodness, which thou hast laid up for them that fear thee, which thou hast wrought for them that trust in thee," Psal. xxxi. 19, 20. When the sight of it afar off, and the taste of it in this wilderness, is of so much virtue, what shall the drinking of that wellhead be, when the soul shall be drowned in it?

As these things are divided,—on the one side, many things, and on the other, one kingdom more worth than all, so are men divided accordingly. On the one hand are the nations and Gentiles, on the other a poor handful. Ye my disciples, "Seek ye," says Christ, "first the kingdom of God, and his righteousness, and all these things," what ye shall eat, and what ye shall drink, or wherewithal ye shall be clothed, "shall be added." For after all these things the Gentiles seek, and your Father knoweth that ye have need of them. "Fear not, little flock, for it is your Father's good pleasure to give you the kingdom," Luke xii. 29, 31. Now this division hath been always in the world. "For many say, (Psal. iv. 6, 7), Who will show us any good?" But they who have their affections gathered in one channel toward one thing, are as it were but one man. But, Lord, "lift thou up the light of thy countenance upon us, thou hast put gladness in my heart more than in the time that their corn and wine increased." Here then is even the course of the world, the way of the multitude. They have their way scattered, their gain lies in many arts. Many things they must seek, because they forsake the one thing necessary. When they forsake the one fountain of living water, they must dig up, and hew out to themselves many broken cisterns, that can hold no water, no one to help another. This is even proclaimed by the conversation of a great part of the world. Do ye not declare this, by your eager pursuit of this world, and the things of it, and your careful thoughts of it, that ye have no mind[17] of eternity, or the kingdom to come? Ye seek nothing but things here, and these do not descend after you. Be persuaded, I beseech you, be persuaded of this, that when ye have your hearts below, that ye are no better, the most part of you, than pagans. Ye have this pretence, that it is necessary to live and follow some calling. It is true indeed. But is it not more necessary to live for ever after death than for a moment? Godliness will not prejudge this life or thy calling, but ye seek after these things, as if ye were to live eternally in this vain world. Ye could toil no more, take no more thought for a million of ages, than ye do now for the morrow. This prejudges and shuts out all thoughts of heaven or hell. Ye are called to a kingdom. This is offered unto you. Will ye be so mad as to refuse it, and embrace the dunghill, and scrape it still together? We declare unto you in his name, who is truth itself, that if ye will be persuaded to be Christians indeed, ye shall have these outward things ye have need of, without care and anxiety, which now ye are tormented for. And for superfluities, what need ye care for them? A reasonable man should despise them, and much more a Christian. If ye would not be as pagans without the church, ye must be sober in these things, mortified and dead unto them. There shall be no real difference between thee and a heathen, in the day of appearing before Christ's tribunal, O Christian, except thou hast denied and despised this world, and sought principally the things that are above. Is Christianity no more, I pray you, but a name? Ye would all be called Christians. Why will ye not be so indeed? For the name will never advantage you, but in the day of judgment it shall be

---

17 That is, no thought of eternity. —Ed.

the greatest accession and weight unto your guiltiness, and also to your judgment. Ye would all now be accounted Christians, but if ye be not so in truth, and in deed, the day will come that ye shall wish from your soul ye had wanted the name also, and had lived among these Gentiles and pagans whose conversation ye did follow. For it shall be more tolerable for the covetous worldly pagan in that day, than the covetous Christian.

Oh that ye were once persuaded that there is an inconsistency in them, who seek these many things, and this one kingdom. "But seek ye first the kingdom of God, and his righteousness," in opposition to the Gentiles seeking of many things. Ye may seek the world, but if ye seek it, seek it as if ye sought it not, if ye use it use it as if ye used it not, or use the world as those who do not abuse it, knowing that the fashion thereof passes away. Certainly ye cannot with all seek grace and glory, 1 Cor. ii. 29, 32. Therefore Christ says to enforce his exhortation, (Matth. vi. 24) "No man can serve two masters, for either he will hate the one, and love the other, or else he will hold to the one, and despise the other; ye cannot serve God and mammon." I fear many of you conceive that this belongs not to you. Those who are not naturally covetous and greedy, who are not still in anxiety and perplexity about the things of the world, will possibly conceive themselves free. Nay, but look upon the division that Christ makes. Was there not many a heathen man among the nations, as free of that covetousness noted among men? Were there not as gallant spirits among them, that cared as little for riches as any of us,—nay, men every way of a more smooth and blameless carriage than the most part of us are? Yet behold the construction that Christ puts on them, "after all these things do the nations seek." I think many of them have declaimed more against the baseness of covetous spirits,[18] than many Christian preachers, and in the very practice of it have outstripped the most part of the Christian world. Yet in the scripture sense, even all these who have cried down the world, are but lovers of it, and of themselves too. How can this be? It is certain every man is composed of desires and breathings after some thing without himself. Some men's desires are more shallow and low than others. One man hath honour in admiration, and may despise riches. Another follows his pleasures and may neglect both these. Nay, possibly a man may be moderate in all these things, so that none can challenge him, and yet he is but a lover of the world. It is the master he serves, and the idol he worshippeth, because no man wants one, or many idols, something to take up his affection and desires. Now though such a man seems moderate in these, in comparison of others whose hearts run more after them, yet, because there is no other thing, that does take up his heart so much as these,

---

18 Quid non mortalia pectora cogis
 Auri sacra fames?
  Virg. Æneid, lib. iii. ver. 56.

"O sacred hunger of pernicious gold!
What bands of faith can impious lucre hold?"
 Dryden's Translation.

Nihil enim est fam angusti animi, tamque parvi, quam amare divitias nihil honestius, magnifi entrusque, quam pecuniam contemnere, si non habeas si habeas, ad beneficentiam liberalitem que conferre. "There is no surer characteristic of a narrow and little mind than to love riches, nothing more amiable and noble than to despise money if you possess it not—if you possess it, to be beneficent and liberal in the use of it." Cic. De Offic. lib. i. cap. 20.—Ed.

he is but in Christ's account among the heathen nations. Some of you are not in great expectations, ye have but mean projects, ye seem content with few things, ye are not vexing yourselves as others do, but let the world come and go as it pleases, without much disquiet. This, I say, may be the temper of some natural spirits, yet I ask such of you, is there any thing else ye seek more after, or spend more time and thought upon, and what is that? Is there any other thing ye are more taken up with, than your present ease and accommodation in this life? No certainly, ye cannot say so, however your projects be mean and low, yet they are confined within time and things present, and the kingdom of grace and glory comes not much in your mind. Then, I say, thou art but a lover of the world. Mammon is thy god. Thou seekest not the kingdom of heaven, and shalt not obtain it. For that which the nations seek after is thy predominant.

Will ye then, I beseech you, gather in your hearts to consider this. Is it a light matter we speak of, life or death? Doth it not concern you as much as you are worth? Therefore consider it as seriously as if you were going hence to be no more. Many of you will not grant worldly mindedness a sin. When ye make it a god, and sacrifice unto it, ye fancy that ye are seeking heaven. I pray you do not deceive your souls. Give them as good measure as ye would do your bodies in any thing. Would ye say ye were seeking after any thing, I suppose to find such a friend to speak to, would ye, I say, think that ye earnestly desired to see that friend, and sought him, if ye did all the day take up your time with other petty business that might be done at any time? How can ye imagine ye seek not the world but heaven, when, if ye would look back upon the current and stream, both of your affections and endeavours, ye would find they have run this way toward your present ease and satisfaction? Ye do not give one entire hour to the thought of Jesus Christ and his kingdom, it may be, in a whole week.

Are ye then seekers of the kingdom? If ye did but examine one day how it is spent, ye might pass a judgment upon your whole life. Do ye seek that first which is fewest times in your thoughts, and least in your affections, and hath least of your time bestowed on it? Alas, do not flatter yourselves. That ye seek first which is often in your mind, which uses to stir up your joy or grief, or desire most. It is this present world only, and this present world is your portion. Ye shall lose the kingdom of heaven by seeking to make the world sure. As for the children of God, ye who will be his disciples, (to such he speaks here,) it becomes not you to be like the heathens. Ye ought, most of all, to adorn your holy profession, your high calling to a kingdom above. If then ye seek these things below, as if ye sought them not, ye ought to make religion your main business, else ye are not indeed religious. If Christianity take not up a man, he hath not the thing, but the name. "Seek first," that is, chiefly, principally, and above all, "the kingdom of God and his righteousness." Nay, this is more strange, it is a first that hath no second. Seek this first, so as if ye sought nothing else, and all things necessary here shall be superadded to the seeking and finding of this kingdom.

This is that which I would have engraven on all our hearts, that there is a necessity of making Christianity our calling and trade, our business and employment, else we must renounce it. It will take our whole man, our whole time, not spare hours, and by thoughts. Ye have a great task to accomplish, a great journey to make. If ye give not all diligence to add to your faith, virtue, knowledge, temperance, patience, godliness, brotherly kindness, and charity, ye are certainly blind, and see not afar off, and have not been purged from your old sins, 2 Pet. i. 5-11. This imports that those who make not religion their great comprehensive study, do neither know eternity, nor see into it. Oh, how may this word strike into the hearts of many Christians, and pierce as a sword! Is our lazy, indifferent, and cold service at some appointed hours, "all diligence"? Or, is it diligence at all? Is there not more diligence and fervour in other things than this, to add grace to grace? Who is covetous of such a game? Are not many more desirous of adding lands and houses to their lands and houses, and money to their stock, than to add to their faith virtue? &c. Who among you is enlarging his desires, as the grave, after conformity to Jesus Christ, and the righteousness of his kingdom, that this treasure of grace may abound? Alas, we are poor mean Christians, because we are negligent! For "the hand of the diligent maketh rich," Prov. x. 4. But we become poor in grace, because we deal with a slack hand. Is there any great thing that is attainable without much pains and sweating? *Difficilia quæ pulchra.*[19]

Think ye to come to a kingdom by sleeping through some custom of godliness? "Seest thou a man diligent in his business? that man shall stand before kings, he shall not stand before mean men," Prov. xxii. 29. This advances him to be a courtier. And is not this business of Christianity more con-

---

19 That is, "It is difficult things that are admired."—Ed.

siderable to be diligent about when it advances a man into the court of heaven, into his presence in whose favour is life, and whose loving kindness is better than life? And not only so, but if ye be diligent here ye shall obtain a kingdom. "Seek first the kingdom of God." "The hand of the diligent shall bear rule but the slothful shall be under tribute," Prov. xii. 24. If ye make this your business, and spend your spirits in it, ye shall be kings and priests with God in the kingdom above, that may suffer many partakers without division or emulation. It is he that overcomes, that shall have the new name, the white raiment, the crown of life, and all the glorious things which are promised to them that overcome in the second and third chapters of the Revelation. O what glad tidings are these! This is the gospel of peace. This is the joyful sound that proclaims unto us so great, so excellent things as a kingdom, the kingdom of God, an everlasting kingdom like God, a kingdom glorious as he is, a kingdom suitable to his royal Majesty, and the magnificence of his palace above. Are we called into this by the gospel, and would ye know what is the sum thereof? It is this. Ho! every one that will have great things, ho! every one that will be a king to God, and to bear rule over kings in the great day, come, here it is, overcome yourselves here in the Lamb that hath overcome, follow Jesus the captain of your salvation, who for the joy and glory which was set before him, despised all the glory of this world, and the pains and shame of the cross, Heb. xii. 1, 2. "Why do ye spend your money for that which is not bread, and your labour for that which satisfieth not?" Isa. lv. 1, 2, 3. All ye toil about, what is it? Children's fancies. Such houses and kingdoms as they build in the sand.

Why spend ye your time and labour upon earthly things that are at an end? Here is a kingdom worthy of all men's thoughts, and affections, and time. The diligent shall have it. Gird up the loins of your mind, and seek it as the one thing needful. Many of you desire this kingdom, but alas! these are sluggard's wishes, ye have fainting desires after it. Your desires consume and waste you. But ye put not forth your hand, and so ye have nothing. "The soul of the sluggard desireth and hath nothing, but the soul of the diligent shall be made fat," Prov. xiii. 4. Do ye see any growing Christian, but he that is much in the exercise of godliness, and very honest in it? See ye any fat souls, but diligent souls? Our barrenness and leanness hath negligence written upon it. Do ye not wonder that we are not fat and flourishing, as palms and cedars in the courts of our God? Certainly it is no wonder. Is it not a wonder that our sleeping away secure, keeps so much as the leaves of a profession upon us? Therefore Christians, let this be your name, Seekers, but seekers of what? Not of any new religion, but of the good old kingdom of God, proponed to us in the gospel. And remember that the seeker must seek diligently, if he think that which he seeks worthy of finding. "He that comes to God must believe that he is, and that he is the rewarder of them that diligently seek him," Heb. xi. 6. Your seeking will proclaim your estimation of what ye seek. It will be written on it, what your desires are. Many men's unfrequent and lazy prayers have this written upon them in legible characters, I care not whether God grant or not. Diligence speaks affection, and affection principles[20] diligence. And if ye be seekers, ye must be so still, till ye find, and

---

20 Excites.—Ed.

have no more want. When ye have done all, ye must stand, Eph. vi. 10, 16. When ye have found all, ye must seek. Ye do but find in part, because the kingdom of God is but coming in the glory and perfection of it. Nay, I believe the more ye find, the more ye will seek, because tasting what this kingdom is, can best engage the affection and resolution after it. Seeking is an exercise suitable to a Christian in this state of pilgrimage. Enjoyment is for his own country, heaven. And shall not the bitterness and pains of seeking, sweeten the enjoyment of this kingdom when it is found? This will endear it and make it precious. Yet it needs no supereminent and accessory sweetness, it is so satisfactory in itself. Christians, remember your name. When you have attained all, still seek more. For there is more to be found here than ye have yet found. It is sitting down on our attainments that makes us barren and lean Christians. Desires and diligence are the vital sap of a Christian. Enlarge once your desires as the grave, that never says I have enough. And ye have good warrant so to do, because that which ye are allowed to desire is without bounds and measure. It is inexhaustible, and when once desires have emptied the soul, and made it capable of such a great kingdom, then let your study be henceforth to fill up that void with this kingdom. Let your diligence come up to desires, and at length ye shall be what ye would be, ye shall find what ye sought.

Sermon IV.

"But seek ye first the kingdom of God," &c.
Matthew vi. 33.

O "seekest thou great things for thyself," says God to Baruch, (Jer. xlv. 5) "seek them not." How then doth he command us in the text to seek a kingdom? Is not this a great thing? Certainly it is greater than those great things he would not have Baruch to seek after, and yet he charges us to seek after it. In every kind of creatures there is some difference, some greater, some lesser, some higher, some lower; so there are some men far above others in knowledge, understanding, strength, and such like. Yet such is the order God hath made, that the lowest angel is above the highest man, so that in comparison of these, the greatest man is but a mean worm, a despisable nothing. Among things created, some are greater, some lesser. "When I consider the heavens, the work of thy fingers," says David, "the moon and stars which thou hast ordained: What is man, that thou art mindful of him? and the son of man that thou visitest him?" Psal. viii. 3, 4. But when all these are compared with God, then the difference of greater and lesser disappears. In the night there are different lights, the moon and stars, "and one star," says Paul, "differeth from another in glory." Some are of the first, some of the second, and most of them the third magnitude. Nay, but let the sun arise—and all these are alike, they are all darkness when compared with the sun's brightness. What then are angels and men to God, who is a light inaccessible and full of glory, whom no eye hath seen or can see? "All nations before him are as nothing, yea, they are counted to him less than nothing, and vanity," Isa. xl. 12-19; 1 Tim. vi. 15, 16. The sun himself shines not before him, and the moon gives not her light. Now is it not so proportionably here? If we stay within the sphere of temporal and worldly things, some are great, some small, some things of greater, some things of less consequence, greater or smaller in their appearance to us, and in men's fancies. But if we go further and look into eternity, then certainly all these will appear small and inconsiderable. This earth seems very spacious, and huge in quantity unto us who dwell upon it. We discern mountains and valleys, sea and land, and do make many divisions of it. But if one man were above where the sun is, and looked down upon the earth, he would consider it but as one point almost invisible, that had no proportion to the vast dimensions of heaven. Even so it is here, while men abide within their own orb, their natural understanding, and do compare time only with time, and temporal things with temporal, riches with poverty, honour with disgrace, pleasure with pain, learning with ignorance, strength with weakness, pleasant lands and goodly houses with wildernesses and wild deserts where none do well. It is no wonder, I think, that those who compare themselves with some that commend themselves, are not wise, 2 Cor. x. 12, 13. There is but one perfect pattern they should look to, if they would not be deceived. While ye stay your thoughts within these bounds, ye apprehend in yourselves great odds between one thing and another. But if once the Spirit of God enlightened your eyes, and made you to see far off, if ye were elevated above your own station, to the watch-tower of the holy scriptures, to behold off[21] these, by the prospect of saving faith, things that are afar off, such as heaven and hell, eternity, salvation and condemnation, O how would all these differences in a present world vanish out of sight, in the presence of these vast and infinite things! Food and raiment are great things to the most part of men, therefore do they toil so much about them, and take so much thought for them, how to feed, and how to be clothed, how to have a full and delicate table, and fine clothes! Again, many others apprehend some greatness and eminency in honour and respect among men; others in pleasure and satisfaction to their senses, even as a beast would judge. Others apprehend some worth and excellence in great possessions, in silver and gold beside them, and have a kind of complacency in these. But if once this kingdom of God entered into your heart, if ye saw the worth of it, the vast dimensions of it, the pleasure, honour, and profit of it, then certainly all other things would appear to be mean and low, not worth a thought beforehand. Advantage and disadvantage would be all one to you. Honour and dishonour, evil report and good report, pleasure and pain, would have no distance from one another; this gain, this honour, this pleasure of the kingdom of God, would so overmaster them, so outshine them.

Nay, I may say, if ye but knew your immortal souls, or your own worth beyond the rest of the creatures, such as silver, gold, lands, houses, &c., I am confident ye would fall in your esteem of

---

21 From these, as from mount Pisgah.—Ed.

them. They would appear but low, base things in regard of the soul. Suppose even this world came in competition, (the gain of it now seems great gain,) but I pray you, if ye laid all that world in the balance with your soul, what would weigh most? Christ holds it forth to a rational man, to judge of it; "What shall it profit a man, if he shall gain the whole world, and lose his own soul, or be cast away?" Would ye account yourselves gainers, when ye have lost yourselves? Matt. xvi. 26; Luke ix. 25. Is not a man better than meat? Are not your souls more precious than the finest gold? When you lose your souls, whose shall these be? "What shall a man give in exchange for his soul?" And if there be no one more to possess or use, what profit is it? This then that we have in hand is one thing of greatest moment and concernment in the world. Let me then beseech you to weigh these things in the balance of the sanctuary,—your souls, and this world, the kingdom of God, and many temporal things, such as food and raiment. Ye never enter into the comparison of these things in your mind. If ye did, would ye not see to which side the balance would turn? Therefore we would have you look upon these words of our Saviour, which are the just balance of the sanctuary. Behold how the question is stated, how the comparison goeth. It is not whether I shall want food and raiment, and other necessary things here, or the kingdom of God hereafter? It is not thus cast—in the one balance, the present life and its accommodations, in the other, the life to come and God's kingdom. Indeed if it were so, without all controversy this kingdom would carry it. I say, if there were an inconsistency supposed between a life here, and a life hereafter, suppose no man can be godly, except he be miserable, poor, naked, afflicted, extremely indigent, yet I say the balance thus casten, would be clear to all men that judged aright. Would not eternity weigh down time? Would not an immortal soul weigh down a mortal body? What proportion would the raiment of wool, or gold, or silk have to the white and clean linen, the robes of righteousness, the robes of saints, and to the crown of glory that fadeth not away? What proportion would our perishing pleasures have to the rivers of pleasures, pure, unmixed, undefiled pleasures at God's right hand for evermore? Would ye thus rate this present span, inch, and shadow of time, if ye considered the endless endurance of eternity? I am sure reason itself might be appealed unto, though faith were not to judge.

Though it would hold well enough so, yet our Lord Jesus Christ states the controversy otherwise, and holds out another balance, that it may be the more convincing and clear, if it were possible even, to overcome natural consciences with the light of it. And it is this, in the one hand you may see food and raiment, things that belong to this life; and, on the other hand, you may behold the kingdom of God, and his righteousness, grace, and glory; and, besides that, even all these other things that ye did see in the other hand, food, raiment, &c., "all these things shall be added."

Wisdom, in the Proverbs, uses such a device to catch poor, foolish, and simple men: "Happy," says Solomon, "is the man that findeth wisdom, and the man that getteth understanding. For the merchandise thereof is better than the merchandise of silver, and the gain thereof than fine gold. She is more precious than rubies: and all the things thou canst desire are not to be compared unto her." Here is the weight of wisdom in itself. See how ponderous it is of itself; so heavy that it may weigh down all that come within the compass of desire, and certainly its compass is infinite. But, he adds, "Length of days are in her right hand, and in her left hand riches and honour. Her ways are ways of pleasantness, and all her paths are peace. She is a tree of life to them that lay hold upon her." She is a tree of life in herself, though she had no accession of other things, "and happy is every one who retaineth her," Prov. iii. 13-19.

Now, O men, if ye will not be allured with the beauty and excellency of the princess, wisdom herself, then, I pray you, look what follows her. That which now ye are pursuing after with much labour and pains, and all in vain too, is here in her train. Look how the comparison is stated. Christ Jesus would catch us with a holy guile, and, if it had success, O! it would be a blessed guile to us. Ye have large and airy apprehensions of temporal things, which ye call needful, and ye cannot behold eternal things. Ye know not the worth of this kingdom. Ye conceive that godliness is prejudicial unto you in this life, that the kingdom of grace will make you miserable here; and that ye cannot endure. Ah, be not mistaken, come and look again. If godliness itself will not allure you, if the kingdom itself will not weigh with you, then, I pray you, consider what an appendix, what a consectary these have. Consider that the sum is added to the principal, which ye so much seek after. But ye refuse the principal, the kingdom. Ye have not right thoughts of godliness, "for godliness is profitable unto all things, having the promise of the life that now is, and that which is to come," 1 Tim. iv. 8. Now, is not this "a faithful saying?" If ye believe it so to be, is it not "worthy of all acceptation?"

Ye may have things necessary here, food and raiment. And if ye seek more, if ye will be rich, and will have superfluities, then ye shall fall into many temptations, snares, and hurtful lusts, which shall drown you in perdition, 1 Tim. vi. 8-11. Nature and reason might check such exorbitances, for nature is content with few things. Therefore believe that "godliness with contentment is great gain." Ye are now only seeking temporal gain, but that is neither great gain, nor gain at all, when ye lose your soul. For that is an irrecoverable and incomparable loss. Ye may have these outward things, God's blessing, and peace with them, and heaven too if ye choose this kingdom before all things, and above all things. But if ye give these other things the preeminence, it is uncertain if ye will get what ye seek, and ye shall certainly be eternal losers beside. If there were no more but this kingdom alone, it might weigh all down. If heaven and earth were laid in a balance, would not heaven, if it were ponderous according to its magnitude, weigh down the earth exceedingly out of sight? Would it not vanish as a point? Even so, though this kingdom of grace and glory were alone, in opposition to all these things that ye take thought for, it would weigh them down eternally. Look what the weight of glory was to Paul, when he says, 2 Cor. iv. 17, "For our light affliction, which is but for a moment, worketh for us a far more exceeding and eternal weight of glory, while we look not at the things which are seen, but at the things which are not seen, for the things which are seen are temporal, but the things which are not seen are eternal." The weight of glory is eternal, and far exceeds any thing temporal. The one scale of the balance goes up, as it were, eternally out of sight, out of thought, the one goes up for lightness and vanity, and the other goeth down, for weight and solidity, out of sight, and out of the thought and imagination. If ye looked upon these things which are invisible and eternal, as Paul did, it would be so with you also.

But when withal the earth and its fulness is in the scale with God's kingdom and righteousness, will not these, with that accession, weigh down the earth alone? Is it food and raiment that ye seek? Then I say, food and raiment is on this kingdom's side also. And ye shall be more sure of these things, because ye have God's promise for them. The wicked have not his word and promise for prosperity, even not so much as to answer their necessities, but only they may sometimes prosper in the world, in his providence. But God's people shall have him engaged in their need for their temporal being here in this world. "O fear the Lord, ye his saints, for there is no want to them that fear him. The young lions do lack and suffer hunger, but they that seek the Lord shall not want any good thing," Psal. xxxiv. 9, 10. Godliness hath the promise of this life. Now, then, ye are more assured of temporal things by these means than any monarch can be. The world's stability depends only upon a command. But your food and raiment here is grounded upon a promise, and though heaven and earth should fail and pass away, yet not one jot of truth shall fail. God indeed may change his command if he pleases, but not his promises. Now, then, let all the world judge, come and see this balance, how on the one hand are food, raiment, and all things needful for this present life, on the other hand, these same thing necessary for our bodies, and well being here, and that more solidly and sweetly flowing from God's love, grounded on a promise,—I think this weighs down already, if we should say no more. But then behold what more is on his right hand. There is a kingdom of God beside, an eternal kingdom, and this weighs down eternally. All this world is but an accession and addition to it. The promises of this life are not your portion and inheritance, they are but superadded to your portion, so then we have as much beside, an inheritance incorruptible and undefiled, as the world have for their inheritance, yea, and more sure and more sweet beside. We might with reverence change that verse which Paul has on this consideration, "If we had hope only in this life, we were of all men most miserable," 1 Cor. xv. 19. He speaks thus because of afflictions and persecutions. But on this consideration we might say, If we have hope in Christ only in this life, we were *not* of all men most miserable, but most blessed, because we have all these things added to us, without toil and vexation, without care and anxiety, by divine promise and providence, with God's blessing and favour, what the world takes thought for, rendeth their hearts for, toils their bodies for, and yet are not sure of success, or if they get them, they get a curse with them.

Now when the balance is thus presented, what is your choice? What will ye seek after? Will ye seek this present world, and lose the kingdom of heaven? Or will ye choose to "seek first the kingdom of God and his righteousness," and then ye shall have in this world what is good for you? The choice is soon made in men's judgments. Ye dare not any of you deny, but it ought thus to be. But who seriously ponders these things till their minds affect their hearts? Who will sit down to meditate upon them, and pass a resolute and well grounded choice upon deliberation? Remember what Christ says, "No man can serve two masters." Ye may indeed have both these things, and the kingdom. But ye cannot seek them both, they are not so consistent. "But seek first the kingdom of God," and then all these things shall be given you.

Now there is no more need of any second seeking. For "all these things shall be added" as an accessory to the first. O see then, ye whose projects and thoughts are towards present things,—ye spend the prime and flower of your affections, and time upon them,—ye cannot also seek the kingdom of heaven. Unless ye seek them as if ye sought them not, ye cannot seek this blessed kingdom. If ye seek not this kingdom as the one thing necessary, and your seeking proclaim that ye account it so, ye do not seek it aright. If ye be careful and troubled about many things, ye proclaim that ye do not think there is but one thing needful, ye do not, like Mary, choose the good part which shall not be taken from you, Luke x. 41, 42. If ye would abandon the distracting care of the world, and let all your anxiety and care vent itself here upon the kingdom of God, all these things would be added besides the kingdom itself. "Seek the kingdom of God *and his righteousness.*" I conceive this is added to make us understand the better what it is, and what is the way to it. The kingdom of God is the kingdom of grace, in which he rules in us by his Spirit. For Jesus Christ is come for this end, and made grace to superabound over the abounding of sin, that as sin reigned unto death, so grace might reign through righteousness unto eternal life by Jesus Christ our Lord (Rom. v. 21), that as sin had a throne in us, so grace might have a throne, and subject the whole man, rendered obedient to that rule of righteousness that he here holds forth in his word. But this kingdom of God also includes the kingdom of glory, wherein these who overcome this world by faith in the Son of God, reign as kings set upon thrones with God the Father of all. Now because the most part, when they heard of the kingdom of God, dreamed of nothing but a state of happiness in heaven, and passed over the way to it, which is holiness, and they thought not upon the kingdom of grace, which is preparatory unto, and disposes us for the kingdom of glory, therefore Christ exhorts us also to seek his righteousness, opposite to the righteousness of the scribes and Pharisees, who satisfied themselves with a mere walk before men. This was man's righteousness but not God's. This righteousness may be also opposed to the rags of our own righteousness, that we seek to cover ourselves with, Isa. lxiv. 6. The apostle says of the Jews, Rom. x. 3, 4, "For they being ignorant of God's righteousness, and going about to establish their own righteousness, have not submitted themselves to the righteousness of God. For Christ is the end of the law for righteousness to every one that believeth."

Now here is the business, and I would have you to conceive it right. The gospel calls you to a kingdom. This is certainly more than all earthly kingdoms. But how shall ye come to it? Not at the nearest hand, not *per saltum*.[22] No, believe it, ye must come and enter this way, before ye compass the end, and the way to this kingdom is by another kingdom, namely righteousness. It is the kingdom of grace within us, and the fruit of it is this. Deny

---

22 That is, not "by a leap."—Ed.

thyself, and follow me, Matt. xvi. 24-26. Overcome yourselves, and your corrupt lusts, and ye shall be more than conquerors. Kingdoms are gotten by conquest. But here is the greatest conquest and triumph in the world, for a man to overcome himself. He that rules himself and his own spirit, is greater than he that taketh a city, Prov. xvi. 32. Other conquerors but overcome men like themselves, and yet are overcome by themselves, and their own passions, and so are but slaves indeed. But if ye deny yourselves, and resign yourselves to Jesus Christ, ye shall be more than conquerors, Rom. viii. 37. This then is the kingdom ye must seek first, and it is the first step to the throne of glory. If ye would have a throne after this life, you must have a throne of grace in your hearts. "If the Son shall make you free, then shall ye be free indeed." They truly are kings who are most subject to God above themselves, and free from the bonds of creatures. This is the glorious liberty of the children of God, to have liberty from him to make sin a captive. It is a righteous kingdom, a kingdom of righteousness. Therefore ye must here study righteousness and holiness, "for the grace of God that hath appeared to all men, and bringeth salvation, teacheth us, that denying all ungodliness, and worldly lusts, we should live soberly, righteously, and godly in this present world looking for the blessed hope, and the glorious appearing of the great God, and our Saviour Jesus Christ," &c. Tit. ii. 11, &c. All men love the salvation it brings. But do ye love the lessons it teaches you? Ye would all be glad to have that blessed hope, and obtain the salvation which the saints look for, when Christ shall appear again in glory. But how few learn and practise what the gospel teacheth, to mortify and deny your corrupt lusts, and live daily in the practice of sobriety, equity, and piety! O if this were engraven upon your hearts, that ye might study to do that in this present world, which this precious grace and gospel teaches us to do in it! Know ye not, brethren, that all your pains in seeking heaven, are not about heaven itself immediately, but the way to it, which is holiness? Without this, no man shall see the Lord, ye need not seek the kingdom of glory, hope for it, and look for it. But seek grace and righteousness in this world, and if ye obtain them, ye have not much to do, but to look for the blessed hope and Christ's glorious appearance to judgment. For if ye have sought and got grace here, Christ will come with grace and glory at the day of his revelation. Will ye consider that ye are redeemed by Christ? But from what is it? From hell only, and eternal death only? No, no, for we are redeemed from all iniquity, as well as the curse of the law and the wrath to come, Matt. i. 21, Tit. ii. 14. This deliverance from sin is the greater and best half of our redemption. Consider also to what ye are redeemed. Is it to happiness and glory only? No certainly, but unto grace also. For Christ "gave himself for us, that he might purify us unto himself a peculiar people, zealous of good works." These things should ministers teach and exhort, and above all things press them upon men's consciences. We are redeemed from all our enemies to serve God without fear, in holiness and righteousness all the days of our life, Luke i. 74, 75. Yea, glory is not glory, except it be complete grace, so we must call the kingdom of glory. If ye believed that it was nigh you, ye would look then for the perfection of grace. And will ye not love the beginning of it here?

But this is not all. There is yet more here to comfort us. Seek the righteousness of God. There is a righteousness of God by faith, manifested in the gospel for lost sinners, who have nothing to cover them. Now I say ye must so seek inherent grace, as ye may not make it your covering, and the only foundation of your confidence. Sinners, the thing which ye first seek and find, is to be clothed with God's righteousness, that he may see no iniquity within you, and then let it be your daily study henceforth to be adorned and made all glorious within, with grace and holiness. Ye must first renounce all your own righteousness, and then be clothed with the robes of God's righteousness, ye must still renounce it, that grace may appear as the gift of God, and not yours; as his beauty, not your ornament. If ye be imperfect in your own righteousness, comfort yourselves in the righteousness of God made yours by faith, that worketh by love and purifies your hearts, for, says the apostle, Gal. ii. 16, 17, Though we are not justified by the works of the law, but by the faith of Christ, yet we must keep ourselves from every wicked thing, and perfect holiness in the fear of God, for if while we seek to be justified by Christ, and we ourselves be found sinners, impenitent and impure, is therefore Christ the minister of sin? God forbid.

Sermon V.

"Seek first the kingdom of God," &c.
Matthew vi. 33.

It may seem strange, that when so great things are allowed, and so small things are denied, that we do not seek them. The kingdom of God and his righteousness are great things indeed, great not only in themselves, but greater in comparison of us. The things of this world, even great events, are but poor, petty, and inconsiderable matters, when compared with these. Yet he graciously allows a larger measure of these great things relating to his kingdom and righteousness, than of those lesser things he hath promised to give his people, and he commands us to seek after these greatest things. "Seek first the kingdom of God, and his righteousness, and all these things shall be added unto you."

This indeed is most suitable to his Majesty, and to us also. It is most becoming his loyal Majesty when he is to declare his magnificence, and to vent his love, to give such high and eminent expressions of it. A kingdom is a fit expression of a king's love and good will. Kings cannot give empires, unless they unking themselves. But Christ is the "King of kings," and hath prepared a kingdom for them that love him. It is a glorious declaration of God's excellent name, that he is good to all, kind even to the evil and unthankful. His tender mercies are over all his works. The whole earth is full of his riches, and the wretched posterity of Adam have the largest share of his goodness, even since the first defection from him. Nay, but there are other things prepared and laid up for them that seek him, O how great is that goodness! How excellent is that loving kindness! Psal. xxxi. 19, 20, Psal. xxxvi. 5, 10. These things have not yet entered into the heart of men to consider. If ye could speak the mind of it, then the tongue could express it. If ye could apprehend the wonders of it, then the heart could conceive it, but this the scripture denies, Isa. lxiv. 4. "For since the beginning of the world, men have not heard nor perceived by the ear, neither hath the eye seen, O God, besides thee, what he hath prepared for him that waiteth for him," or as Paul writes, "Eye hath not seen, nor ear heard neither have entered into the heart of man, the things which God hath prepared for them that love him. But God hath revealed them unto us by his Spirit, who searcheth all things, even the deep things of God," &c., 1 Cor. ii. 7-14. Is not a kingdom a gift suitable to such a Giver? And is not this kingdom of God every way like himself? These things are prepared by Christ, and there is no more to do, but to give to him that asks, and he that seeks shall find. This righteousness, divine and human, is it not wholly of God's finding out? Is it so glorious, so excellent, as to hide the greatest spots of the creation from his spotless eyes? For even hell itself is naked before him, and destruction hath no covering, even the heavens are not pure in his sight, he chargeth his angels with folly, Job xxvi. 6, chap. iv. 17, 18, 19, chap. xv. 14-17. When all the creatures could not procure the salvation of sinful men, when the depth said, it is not in me, and the sea said, it is not with me, and the heavens and heights said so too,—even angels could not redeem us,—the redemption of the soul was so precious, it would have ceased for ever, if divine wisdom had not found it out, and almighty power brought it to pass. "Sacrifice and offering thou wouldest not, but a body hast thou prepared for me. Lo, I come, in the volume of the book it is written of me, I delight to do thy will, O my God, yea thy law is within my heart," Psal. xl. 6, 7, 8, Heb. x. 5-11. All this was with God, and he knew the way thereof. Christ framed this royal robe of his righteousness, by suffering and death, which may cover all our nakedness. He came and sought the human nature with all its infirmities. He became in all things like unto us, sin only excepted. On him God laid our iniquities. For he himself "bare our sins in his own body," when he was slain upon the cross or tree, "that we, being dead unto sin, might live unto righteousness," 1 Pet. ii. 24, 2 Cor. v. 21. Behold what a wonder! Iniquities, and our iniquities, laid upon the immaculate Lamb, Jesus Christ. Our Redeemer hid his divinity, his holiness, and his innocence, as with a vail and covering from the eyes of God's awful justice. He smites the Shepherd, his beloved Son, as he did the rebel creature. It pleased the Father to bruise him and put him to grief, when his soul was made an offering for sin, Isa. liii. 4-11, Zech. xiii. 7. Justice did not look through the covering to his innocence, but reckoned and numbered him among transgressors, when he bore the punishment of our sins, and made an atonement for them, Isa. liii. 11, 12, Gal. iii. 13, 14.

Now hence it is that the righteousness of Jesus Christ, which he learned in the days of his flesh, and purchased by his death, is prepared for us, to put on. "Whosoever will, let him come and take it." Empty yourselves, stripped naked of all kind of coverings but sin and unworthiness, that which God's holy eye cannot behold, and seek Christ's righteousness to adorn and cover you. Behold it shall hide all your sins and abominations, of whatsoever nature and degree, from the pure and unspotted eyes of God's justice, which are as a flaming fire, to consume what it cannot look upon without abhorrence. Put on this righteousness of God, and justice shall not draw by the covering, to look under it. It shall look upon the sinner as a righteous man on the slave of Satan as a child of God, on the heir of hell as the heir of heaven, if he sincerely repent of, and forsake his sins, believe in Christ and obey his gospel. "Behold all things are new, and all things are of God, who hath reconciled the world unto himself by Jesus Christ," &c., 2 Cor. v. 17-19, Col. i. 19-24. Christ was no worse dealt with for our sins, than we shall be well dealt with for his righteousness. This is the gift of God. And is it not worthy to be sought? Is it not a gift worthy of him to give? Is it not also suitable for us to ask? "If thou knewest the gift of God, and who it is that saith to thee, Give me to drink, thou wouldst have asked of him, and he would have given thee living water," &c. John iv. 10-15. So say I to you, if ye knew the gift of God, what this kingdom is, what this righteousness is, and who is appointed by God to be the treasure house of all fulness, to be communicated to us, ye would certainly ask of him the water of life. Ye would surely seek this kingdom of God and his righteousness. He doth not value other things. God only hath these things offered in the gospel, in choice of many, therefore are they laid up for some few, whom he makes his peculiar treasure and jewels, Mal. iii. 17, Exod. xix. 5, 6. If ye knew a monarch that was a possessor of all this habitable world, and was about to express his singular affection towards some persons, if his kingdom or the half or whole of it was not sufficient, to be a token of it, but he had found out some other thing, and laid it up for them, and distributed the kingdom, the lands and cities among others, certainly ye would think that behoved to be some strange thing of great price. If the Lord was pleased to give you abundance of all things here, make you all great, rich, and honourable persons, then many would seek no other expression of his love. They would think he did well enough to them. But alas! what is it all? He esteems it so little that he often casts it to swine, the profane and wicked world. He fills their belly with his hid treasure, Psal. xvii. 14. He makes his sun to shine, and his rain to fall on the evil and the good, Matt. v. 45. It is a demonstration that it is but a base thing, when it is so common, I mean, in comparison of the portion of his saints. For though these worldly things are good in themselves, yet they are not precious, they are not pearls. Would he cast pearls before dogs and swine? The honourable man's brutishness and ignorance of God may demonstrate to you he cares not for it. "The Most High ruleth in the kingdom of men, and giveth it to whomsoever he will," and sometimes "setteth up over it the basest of men," Dan iv. 13-18. If God loved riches well, do ye think he would give them so liberally, and heap them up upon some base covetous wretches? Surely no. But here is the precious thing that is laid up and treasured. The world and its gain seems great, and big in your eyes, ye cannot imagine more, nor wish for more. But alas! how low and base spirits have ye! It is but as the dunghill that the swine feed on, or the husks which the prodigal desired to feed his belly with, when he began to be in want, Luke xv. 13-17. So are all men's worldly pleasures, preferments, and profits. But here are some particular things, that only deserve to be called good, namely, "the kingdom of God and his righteousness." And when God had searched the whole world, (to speak with reverence of his glorious Majesty, who needs not inquire into secret things,) when he had looked through all the works of his hand, he sets these apart from all the rest, to be given to the men whom the King shall honour. This kingdom is the substance and accomplishment of heaven's eternal counsel and purpose of grace, which was given in Christ before the world, and it is the end of the Son's redemption of a sinful world, and his intercession for them at God's right hand. "Father," says he, (John xvii. 24), "I will that those whom thou hast given me, be with me where I am, that they may behold the glory which thou hast given me," and for other things he makes them as the stones of the field.

Now I say, as this kingdom of God and his righteousness are suitable expressions of his love, according to his magnificence, so they are also suited to our condition and necessities. No question but he would permit us to seek great things in this world, if these things were really great and good, and if they did become such great immortal spirits as we have. Your souls are above all these things. But this kingdom, and this only, is above the soul. Now then, if ye go out to seek these earthly things, ye must go down from the throne of eminency that God hath set your souls upon by creation, and abuse your spirits by stooping to the very dust of your feet, to embrace these things, and, which is worse, ye put yourselves out of that high throne of dignity that ye are exalted to by Christ's redemption, which we may call a second creation. Jesus declared by the infinite ransom he gave, when he offered himself a sacrifice without spot to God, (Heb. ix. 14) and laid down his life for us, what the worth of your souls was. "None of them," saith the Psalmist, "can by any means redeem his brother, nor give to God a ransom for him, for the redemption of their soul is precious, and it ceaseth for ever," Psal. xlix. 6-10. Call and assemble all the creatures in heaven and earth, summon gold, silver, precious stones, houses, cities, kingdoms, places of trust and dignity, great learning and parts, and every other thing ye can imagine, let them all convene in a parliament, and consult how men shall be ransomed. All of them combined together, though they make one purse, cannot do it. They cannot pay the least farthing. The Lord Jesus Christ then stepped in here, "Lo, I come," — I give the body thou gave me, my life for theirs, "I delight to do thy will, thy law is in my heart."

Are your souls then exalted to such great dignity? Is such a price set upon them, and will ye spend them, for that which could not pay the price for them, "for that which profiteth not?" Ye must go out of yourselves to seek happiness. Then I pray you, go not downward. It is not there, but misery is there. And by going down to the creatures, ye have found it, and cannot lose it to this day. But the kingdom of God is the only thing above. Go up to it. "Seek these things that are above," Col. iii. 1-4. "If then ye be risen with Christ," through the faith of God's operation, "set your affection on things above, where Christ sitteth at God's right hand, and not on things on the earth." These things are but great in your apprehension. If they are at all great indeed, it is only in evil. If then ye seek great things for yourselves, ye may find evil things, ye shall certainly find such evil things as shall drown you in everlasting destruction. "They that will be rich" (in worldly things), who lay up treasures for themselves, and are not rich towards God, "fall into temptation, and a snare, and into many foolish and hurtful lusts which drown men in perdition. For the love of money is the root of all evil, which while some coveted after, they have erred from the faith, and pierced themselves through with many sorrows," 1 Tim. vi. 9, 10. Great things in this world are not always good. To seek them, makes them certainly evil and hurtful. It is not so hurtful to have them, though very dangerous, but it is hurtful, yea, present ruin to seek them. But here is a kingdom that is great, and great in goodness, every way answerable to our necessities. This is the kingdom we should seek above all things.

We would therefore beseech you to be wanters in yourselves, and seekers in Christ, and seekers ye cannot be till ye be wanters, and finders ye cannot be except ye seek in Jesus all satisfaction and remedy of your necessity. This is even the very nature of a Christian, his chief exercise and employment. What then is a Christian's principal study, his great business, his important calling, and what is his success in it? He is a seeker by his employment, or calling here, and he shall certainly find what he asks. But what puts him to seeking? The discovery of his own emptiness, and God's fulness. Therefore study these things most, if ye would be Christians in truth and in deed. It is these two that ye must still pass between, if ye keep them not both in your view at once, ye cannot well perceive any of them, either comfortably, humbly, or profitably.

This is even the sum of Christianity. Look what ye want in yourselves, and make up that in God. Discover your own emptiness and fill it up with God's fulness. "The liberal soul shall be made fat, and he that watereth, shall be watered also himself," Prov. xi. 25. Be not niggards here. Be liberally minded, both in seeking and receiving, so shall ye please him best who counts it his glory to give. "The instruments of the churl are evil, but the liberal deviseth liberal things, and by liberal things he shall stand," Isa. xxxii. 7, 8. Seek answerable to your own necessity, and God's all sufficiency, and know no other rule or measure.

Now, Christians, this is your calling and employment here, to be seekers of God's kingdom and righteousness. But shall we come speed? Yes certainly. It is so far put out of question here, that it needs not be expressed. "Seek first the kingdom of God, and all these things shall be" superadded to you. He thinks it needless to say, *and ye shall find the kingdom of God, and his righteousness*, for it is supposed as a thing unquestionable, and he adds these words, "and all these things shall be added to you," to answer the faithlessness of these who could not credit him in temporal things, though they had concredited[23] to him their immortal souls. Ye do not doubt, then, but ye shall have the kingdom of heaven. Ye do indeed seek it. Many by seeking kingdoms lose here—by seeking to make them more sure, they lose the hold

---

23 Intrusted.—Ed.

they have. Many by aspiring to greater things, lose these things they have, and themselves too. But here is the man that is only sure of success,—the man that may reckon upon his advantage before he take pains, if indeed he resolves to take pains for it. This one thing is made sure, eternal life, if ye lay hold on it here by faith, and quit your hold of present things that end in death, Rom. vi. 21. We may well submit to the uncertainty of all other things, as David, who held himself well satisfied with the everlasting covenant God had made with him, which was well ordered in all things and sure, 2 Sam. xxiii. 5. Though the kingdom and house go, it matters not, if he keep this fast. If he take not away his loving kindness, this is all my comfort, my joy, and my desire. Comfort yourselves with this, amidst the manifold calamities and revolutions of times. Ye see no man can promise himself immunity, or freedom from common judgments. Here ye have no continuing city. Why then do ye not seek one to come, and comfort yourselves in the hope of it? Your rights and heritable securities will not secure your lands and riches for any considerable time. Therefore seek an eternal and sure inheritance, sure mercies. Seek that which ye cannot miss, and having found, cannot lose. Nothing here can you expect either to find, or keep, until ye have found it.

But besides all this, there is an accession to the inheritance. All needful things shall be added, ye shall want "no good thing," Psal. lxxxiv. 11. Will not all this double gain and advantage recompense, yea, overcome all the labours of seeking? Shall it not drive away the remembrance of them? Here then is the most compendious and comprehensive way to have your desires in this life granted, to get your necessities supplied. "Seek first the kingdom of God" and ye shall have them. But if ye seek these things and not heaven, ye shall want this kingdom. I think then it is all the folly and madness in the world, not to take this way, for it is the way to be blessed here and hereafter. And if we choose any other way, it brings no satisfaction here, and it brings eternal misery hereafter. If ye would be well in this world, seek heaven. Do not think that ye should have heaven, or seek God's kingdom from this sordid principle, that ye shall have all worldly things given you, which God pleaseth to bestow. For now man can seek the kingdom of heaven aright, but he that seeks it for itself. Yet if they were no more to proclaim the madness of men, this would sufficiently suffice, all they can desire or expect is promised with the kingdom, and yet they will not seek it.

www.ingramcontent.com/pod-product-compliance
Lightning Source LLC
Chambersburg PA
CBHW030131100526
44591CB00009B/602